THEN & NOW®

PACIFICA

An early touring car pauses at a dusty Edgemar crossroad, probably the intersection of Clifton Road and Hog Ranch Road (later named Waterford Street after most of it was replaced by the Highway 1 freeway). (Courtesy of Nick Gust.)

PACIFICA

Kathleen Manning and Jerry Crow

Library of Congress Control Number: 2009939079

Published by Arcadia Publishing
Charleston, South Carolina

Printed in the United States of America

Then and Now is a registered trademark and is used under license from
Salamander Books Limited

For all general information contact Arcadia Publishing at:
Telephone 843-853-2070
Fax 843-853-0044
E-mail sales@arcadiapublishing.com
For customer service and orders:
Toll-Free 1-888-313-2665

Visit us on the Internet at www.arcadiapublishing.com

ON THE FRONT COVER: This Ocean Shore Railroad car sits on the berm at what was then San Pedro Beach, ready to make its return to San Francisco. Today hardy residents live in the shadow of the old railroad right-of-way at Linda Mar Beach, so named after Andy Oddstad developed the Linda Mar district in the early 1950s. (Then photograph courtesy of the Pacific Historical Society; now photograph by the authors.)

ON THE BACK COVER: Nearly all of the buildings in west Rockaway Beach have been replaced or simply removed since the 1950s. Ben's Trading Post was in the building that had previously been Jim's Pavilion for dancing and Rockaway Beach Mission Catholic Church. Later, Ben's moved to the Linda Mar Shopping Center. The modern photograph was taken on a Wednesday, as indicated by the temporary booths of the thriving farmers market along Old County Road. (Photograph by Frank Gittings.)

CONTENTS

ACKNOWLEDGMENTS

Many of the vintage photographs in this book were previously published in Arcadia's Images of America: *Pacifica*, by Chris Hunter. Our thanks to the *Pacifica Tribune* and the Pacifica Historical Society, Chris Hunter, and Bill Drake for the use of those images. For the other Then images, our thanks to:

Bruce Walker (pages 11, 16, 40, 56, 62)
Ray Higgins (12)
Metha McDavid (17)
? MacDonald (an early developer whose first name is unknown) (23, 46, 53)
Bob Seibert (26, 33, 35)
U.S. Army (36, 43)
Shirlee Gibbs (37)
Eileen Kewnig (38)
Robin Gaio (39)
CalTrans (42)
B. A. Lang (45)
Dan Peters (50)
U.S. Coast Guard (51)
Lee Forster (52)
Lloyd Easterby (68, 76, 77)
Jack W. Chaplin (72)
Alice Blankfort (78)
Joe Fulford (90)

The modern photographs were taken by the authors.

Special thanks to Connie Brown, Charlise Heiser, Steve Merring, and Bill Hall. Sandy Cavallaro was indispensable, both for her long hours of skillful efforts and her unfailing good-humored patience in formatting and organizing the materials for this book.

INTRODUCTION

Our purpose, in addition to showing what things were like in the community decades ago, is to illustrate the specific changes brought about by certain significant influences occurring in the city, in neighboring cities, and in the world beyond. These include the arrival and departure of the Ocean Shore Railroad, coastal bluff erosion, community expansion following World War II and the Korean War, national defense during the cold war, passage of the California Coastal Act, California highway policy, open space legislation, and incorporation of Pacifica.

Pacifica's history began slowly. Few Native Americans actually lived right on the coast. Spanish explorers discovered San Francisco Bay from atop Sweeney Ridge. Irish and Italian immigrants brought their agricultural skills, having been attracted by the climate and proximity to San Francisco. Pacifica became a thriving agricultural area of scattered farms specializing in vegetables and enjoyed the largest artichoke production in the United States in the 1890s.

In 1906, the newly built Ocean Shore Railroad began to cross over the mountains and proceed down the coastal area now known as Pacifica. The railroad builders realized that the produce of the area could be carried to San Francisco in hours rather than the days formerly required by wagons pushing through rugged terrain and rough trails to San Francisco.

It was soon apparent that the beautiful but little-known coast would attract seaside visitors and, yes, even settlers. To that end, stations were built at several stops, where the railroad's salesmen began to sell building lots. These stops and stations became the nucleus for several settlements that later joined together. The railroad operation lost money, but the real estate arm was profitable, as visitors to the coast liked what they saw and began moving to this magnificent area.

The railroad folded in 1920, after the automobile became the preferred method of transportation. The Ocean Shore tracks were paved over by Highway 1, bringing even greater numbers of visitors and settlers. Many bars and clubs were built to entertain the holiday-makers. During the Prohibition era, these bars were turned into "blind pigs" and spots for unloading Canadian liquor. Sheltered beaches and coves provided perfect landing spots lor illegal goods.

World War II was a busy time on the coast as gun emplacements and observation posts were built to help defend the entrance to San Francisco Bay. As the cold war developed, the defense sites were converted to anti-aircraft missile installations even as the area became part of peninsular suburbia.

The city known as Pacifica was incorporated in 1957, when nine small villages joined together. At the time of incorporation, the city contained almost 30,000 people. Today the population is around 39,000. It's not that people don't want to live there; on the contrary, they do. Expansion has been limited because much of the vacant land is set aside as parks or is owned by conservation groups that want to preserve open space. Pacifica is fortunate that it retains its distinctive character and hasn't become just another suburb.

This book illustrates some of the changes in Pacifica throughout the years. Through the juxtaposition of vintage and modem photographs, readers will discover new life in a familiar town.

CHAPTER 1

PACIFIC MANOR

Pacific Manor includes the first housing development along the north San Mateo County coast, Edgemar, plus Fairmont, Fairmont West, and Pacific Heights. Although rural in the 1890s, it was home to the original San Pedro School near Hickey Boulevard and Skyline Boulevard. In *John Barleycorn*, author Jack London credits his teacher there with awakening his love of books. He also mentions some of the lively doings at the Morrisey ranch house, which still exists on Monterey Road.

The first wave of farmers to settle along the San Mateo north coast in the 1860s were Irish farmers who planted mainly potatoes in the sandy soil. This crop flourished for a time but was wiped out by blight in the late 1800s. Beginning in the 1880s, Italian farmers followed and introduced crops such as artichokes, brussels sprouts, and cabbage, all of which did very well in the often-foggy coastal climate. Today the Manor Plaza Shopping Center and adjacent commercial areas occupy much of the area formerly devoted to crops.

Dollaradio was later renamed Globe Wireless. The transmitting station along with its antennae was located on a hill near the receiving station. Many changes have occurred to the area over the years, and the Globe Wireless entity is long gone from California, although it still exists as Globe Telecom, a division of communications giant BayanTel in the Philippine Islands.

Pacific Manor School was originally built on a parcel with part of the Ocean Shore Railroad right-of-way running through the playground. When the school was modernized in 2005, the Pacifica School District acquired clear title to the right-of-way in order to build more classrooms on the site, which it renamed Ocean Shore School.

Hog Ranch Road was a twisting link between Colma, a former center of numerous hog ranches, and coastal farms for many decades. During dense fogs, passengers often stepped out to guide their drivers around the tricky curves. In 1958, construction of the Edgemar Freeway (since renamed in honor of Louis J. Papan, former California assemblyman) replaced the torturous old road with a few sweeping curves. This section of State Highway 1 still retains the breathtaking view that opens before drivers as they first come over the ridge north of town.

In 1926, Capt. Robert Dollar established Dollaradio, the first private-sector worldwide wireless radio network, to maintain communications with his expanding fleet of ocean liners. Regarded by professional maritime telegraphers as having the best wireless reception on the West Coast, this Dollaradio receiving station was the link with Little America, the United States' base in Antarctica, over which came the first word that Adm. Richard Byrd had successfully flown over the South Pole on November 29, 1929. The building has been expanded into a residence and remains overlooking the Pacific Ocean.

This 1942 view of the Manor District is looking down from the corner of Farallone Avenue and Channing Way toward the Pacific Ocean. In the distance near today's Ocean Shore School, there are wooden army barracks—part of the World War II coastal defense system. The large stretches of open, sandy land were ideal for the cultivation of artichokes and brussels sprouts. Today's view shows a totally urbanized metropolitan area with the same breathtaking ocean view.

The bluffs in the northern third of Pacifica are particularly susceptible to erosion by wave action. Over many centuries, the coast has retreated at an average rate of 3 inches per year. The local bluffs are mostly stable, but especially fierce storm seasons undercut significant pieces of ground. Seawalls of large boulders have done much to retard this process, as is shown by the comparison of damage done in 1983 at Pacific Skies Estates and the condition of the same bluff now.

The houses along the west side of Esplanade Drive have a wonderful view of the Pacific Ocean and sunsets. Unfortunately, they rest on a bluff that has repeatedly been undermined by storm waves. By 1990, the distance between their back doors and the bluff edge had been reduced from about 100 feet to only 30 to 50 feet. Storms during the 1998 El Niño advanced the erosion so much that five homes were destroyed. Since then, the base of the bluff has been stabilized using large boulders, and a narrow park has been built where houses once stood.

Wild Bill Nash and his son Frank opened the Coastside Barber Shop on May 1, 1956. Bill discovered that he liked Pacifica while out motorcycling from his home in Martinez. At right, father and son greet Leo Ryan in 1968 during his campaign for the U.S. House of Representatives. Front and center is a young Jackie Speier, who now holds the seat. Today's picture above shows the ever-popular Frank Nash, still the proprietor of the Coastside Barber Shop.

An early Miss Pacifica is being presented with a salami by the Blanda family on the occasion of the opening of the Roma Italian Deli in 1966 at Manor Shopping Center. Today the deli tradition is carried on by the Colombo family, who has owned Colombo's Italian Deli in this same spot since 1986. Today's Miss Pacifica, Azure Armstrong, is greeting, from left to right, Emil Colombo Jr., his wife, Doris, and his parents, Emil Sr. and Kathy.

Save More Meats is a Pacifica institution, second only to Nick's in longevity. In 1955, George Lee noticed a new shopping center being built in Manor and thought it would be a great place for a butcher shop. He and his wife, June, thought Pacifica would be a good place to do business and raise a family. Today their thriving business is in the capable hands of two sons, Kevin (below, left) and Matthew (below, right), who proudly carry on the family tradition.

SHARP PARK

Inhospitable sand dunes characterized the level stretch between Mussel Rock at the northern boundary of present-day Pacifica and Mori Point. The indigenous Ohlones regarded the area as too sandy and windy to make good home sites. They apparently had no coastal settlements between Tmigtac, a small site near the intersection of Reina Del Mar Avenue and Highway 1, and the large village that existed near the site of Mission Dolores in San Francisco. However, the district became the focus of big development dreams as the Ocean Shore Railroad created better access to coastal beaches and space. Those dreams did not materialize for many years, but now there are neighborhoods and the Sharp Park Golf Course in place of the bleak dunes.

Of the three major structures in the old photograph—McCloskey's Castle, Anderson's Store and the Salada Beach railroad station—only the first two remain. The widening of Highway 1 when the freeway portion was extended south through Sharp Park required the demolition of an entire shopping strip from about Paloma Avenue to Eureka Drive.

Beginning in 1905, the Ocean Shore Railroad opened the coastal beaches to city dwellers eager for vacation cottages and weekend day trips away from urban bustle. Troubled by major damage during the 1906 earthquake, by unstable conditions along the awesome coastal route, and by the advent of competition from automobiles and trucks, the railroad ceased operations in 1920. The tracks were taken up and sold along with the rolling stock and other assets. Since then, the company has existed only to gradually sell off its real estate assets.

Brighton Station stood near the intersection of Lakeside Avenue and Francisco Boulevard. Other Ocean Shore Railroad stations in Pacifica were: Mussel Rock (Daly City), Edgemar at Clifton Avenue, Salada at San Mateo (now Paloma) Avenue, Vallemar at Reina Del Mar Avenue (still standing), Rockaway just north of Rockaway Beach Avenue, Fleming on San Pedro Beach about even with Anza Drive, and Tobin at the end of Danmann Avenue. Now a residential complex occupies the site.

SHARP PARK

This Quonset hut was originally constructed in the 1930s as part of the State Relief Camp on the eastern part of the property donated to San Francisco by the terms of the will of Honora Sharp. The camp was administered by San Francisco as a refuge for indigents during the Great Depression. During World War II, it became a detention center for those feared to be potential enemy agents. With the return to peacetime, the detention center was replaced by archery and firearms ranges. The relocated hut is now a childcare center in Pomo Park.

Developer Ray Higgins built this early shopping center to gather many of the businesses that had been spread out along Highway 1 under one roof. This building and the rest of the former businesses shown elsewhere in the Sharp Park Shopping District were displaced when Highway 1 was extended farther south. Nearby Eureka Square Shopping Center now offers the convenience envisioned by Higgins.

Gypsy Hill, possibly named for sojourning travelers in times past, is much more forested now thanks largely to the efforts of Dr. Sebastian Campagna (deceased) and his family. The intended future site of a Coptic Christian retreat, it affords some beautiful coastal views. The portion of the old Sharp Park shopping strip in the lower part of the older photograph was replaced by the widened Highway 1 and the Eureka Square Shopping Center.

Pacifica's current city hall was originally the third San Pedro School on the coast. When the student body outgrew the building, classes expanded into the Sunday school classrooms in the Little Brown Church. With further growth, classes were moved to the new Sharp Park School a quarter-mile to the north. The building owner, developer Ray Higgins, first made it available to nonprofit organizations, then later donated it as city hall in 1958. It looks much the same today as it did on dedication day.

The old Sharp Park Firehouse on the northeast corner of Santa Maria and Palmetto Avenues had a hose drying and rescue drill tower that served during World War II as a duty station for volunteers scanning the sea and sky for possible enemy activity. The volunteers, many of them Boy Scouts, were given the additional duty of putting up street signs on corners where they were lacking. Now a small shopping center occupies the site vacated by the fire department upon completion of the Linda Mar station in 1975.

Sharp Park School was built in 1950 to accommodate new families taking advantage of college benefits for veterans of World War II. In 1953, two wings were added to consolidate classes from overcrowded San Pedro School and other scattered locations. On moving day, the San Pedro School students walked in a double column up Palmetto Avenue to the new school at Bella Vista and Palmetto Avenues. Sharp Park School has since been almost totally rebuilt as Ingrid B. Lacy Middle School.

Knowing that the Ocean Shore Railroad was doomed, developers still hoped to see a busy coastside vacation community in the Brighton Beach and Salada Beach districts. Brighton Beach extended from Mori Point Road to Brighton Avenue, Salada Beach from Brighton Avenue to Paloma Avenue. Ocean Shore Railroad president H. Downey Harvey built two prototype vacation cottages on Salada Avenue in 1920. The cottages look much the same today, although one has had a recent face lift and the other has an addition to one side.

Beach Boulevard was not the originally intended surfside road in Sharp Park; old realtor's maps show another block further west that is under water now. The seawall along Beach Boulevard was protected from the waves by an additional barrier of boulders in the 1950s. Thanks to periodic strengthening of the seawall by Pacifica's public works department, Beach Boulevard remains intact.

This simply constructed building was originally the Salada Hotel. Dating from 1910, it was temporary home to many of the developers and workmen who came down the coast to launch what was expected to be a thriving coastal resort on the scale of Atlantic City, New Jersey, complete with two elaborate casinos on the edges of Laguna Salada. When the resort dream fizzled, the building housed a series of businesses, the most recent being an upholstery shop.

Pacifica's hills have been part of the national defense infrastructure since before World War II. Two observation bunkers and a pair of 6-inch cannons on Milagra Ridge helped protect the entrance to San Francisco Bay. Missiles installed in the 1950s protected against potential Russian air raids until the 1970s. The missile control point was on Sweeney Ridge. The Milagra Ridge storage bunkers and hoist were deactivated in 1974. Now part of the Golden Gate National Recreation Area, Milagra Ridge is a model of successful native habitat restoration.

This house on Brighton Road in West Sharp Park was the first Pacifica home for the Gibbs family. Purchased in 1956 for $13,500, it was considered a higher-end house. It had three bedrooms, one bathroom, and came equipped with either turquoise or gold appliances. As the population grew, all the vacant flat land was filled. Many chose the hillsides for the view of the ocean. Today this is still an area of well-maintained and desirable homes.

This craftsman bungalow at 217 Paloma Avenue was built in 1910 by early settler, John Kewnig, who died in 1918. The family lived there until the late 1930s and traded across the street at Anderson's Store. Later it became a doctor's office. When the need for a high school became an issue, this area was selected for Oceana High School. Three blocks of old homes on Paloma were taken by eminent domain, including this early masterpiece.

The Fahey family was one of the first to farm the fields below Milagra Ridge in the area formerly known as Carmel Valley. Crops grown in the area included artichokes, green peas, and green beans. The area is now known as East Sharp Park. The Fahey barn is gone, the farmhouse has been expanded, and the fields have become a residential neighborhood and Pomo Park.

The clubhouse for the Sharp Park Golf Course was designed by the Willis Polk firm, noted San Francisco architects, and was completed in 1931. Three small murals commissioned by the Works Progress Administration to help support the unemployed during the Great Depression adorn doorways in the bar and dining room. The building is listed as a historic landmark by the City of Pacifica, and the San Francisco Recreation and Parks Department involved the Pacifica Historical Society in design review when the banquet room was added.

The Sixth Tee Inn at Palmetto Avenue and Clarendon Road offered refreshments to golfers as they rounded the turn at the north end of the golf course. The building actually preceded the golf course, having been built in the 1920s, when bathhouses lined Laguna Salada. When the course was first fenced, thirsty players bewailed the loss of their oasis, so a special gate was installed. Later replaced by an apartment complex by developer Andres Oddstad, the new structure included a café so that Sixth Tee Inn proprietress Mrs. Floyd Guffin would still have a living.

A plan to build a grid of freeways on the peninsula (Highways 101, 280, and 1 running north to south and the section of 280 along the San Francisco-Daly City line, 380, and 92 running east to west) included this interchange at Mori Point. The plan was stopped by a grassroots effort. Today what would have been the interchange is occupied by Pacifica's wastewater treatment plant and part of the Golden Gate National Recreation Area.

From 1954 to 1974, the San Francisco Bay Area was protected from possible air attack by a ring of Nike anti-aircraft missile sites. The control site on Sweeney Ridge, now in ruins, had the mission of detecting incoming enemy bombers and of controlling the missiles launched from Milagra Ridge. The facility became obsolete with the invention of inter-continental ballistic missiles impossible to intercept with the technology of the day. National defense strategy then became that of massive retaliation, or Mutually Assured Destruction (MAD).

Laura Briggs originally built this Beach Boulevard structure in the early 1900s and later installed the Japanese Tea Garden building from the 1915 San Francisco Fair behind it as her home. The spot became know as Hazel's Inn in the 1940s and 1950s. Through the years, it was a popular bar and restaurant, and later it became an early gay bar. The business eventually failed, and in the late 1950s the building became the Coastside Bait and Tackle Shop—a mecca for striped bass fisherman. In the mid-1960s, it was burned down after being condemned. Today there is a condominium complex in its place.

The Sharp Park shopping district had many conveniences: markets; a post office; a library; a service station; a dress shop; restaurants; and sporting goods, variety, hardware, and toy stores. Developer Ray Higgins later consolidated some of them under a single roof called Sharp Park Center. The state acquired the stores along this strip under the right of eminent domain for the widening of Highway 1. In 1972, the California Department of Transportation had indicated agreement with an idea to build stores over the freeway similar to downtown Reno, but costs stalled the project.

The broad fields of the area north of Laguna Salada had been created out of desolate dunes around 1900. The low-berm profile between the lagoon and the ocean caused frequent additions of brine. The surface area of the lagoon was reduced when it was deepened as part of the golf course project. The nearest fields in the vintage photograph are now part of the Oceana High School campus.

The U.S. government built the Sharp Park Detention Center on the grounds of the Depression-era relief camp east of the Sharp Park Golf Course. Certain German, Italian, and Japanese persons were held here while their security status was being determined. A rifle range that replaced the wartime buildings has been deactivated pending environmental remediation. An archery range remains active.

This view of Salada Mercantile Company (Anderson's Store) around 1909 shows how Paloma Avenue was enhanced with curbs, young trees, and a sidewalk to attract buyers to the Salada Beach real estate office in the foreground. McCloskey's castle and the large Victorian home built by a Mr. Dennison in 1907 can just be seen in the upper right corner. In the modern photograph, mature trees obscure much of the view, a freeway overpass has replaced the former row of little trees, and the real estate office has been rotated 90 degrees and enlarged.

The stables at Mori's Point stood beside Horse Corral Pond in 1959. After Mori's Point Inn faded, the stable grew shabby. For a while a go-cart course occupied the ground; old tires were used to ring the course and soften the impact of mini-crashes. The stable buildings were torn down years ago, and the tires and other debris were cleaned up over the last few years by Golden Gate National Recreational Area staff and volunteers.

The Pacifica Municipal Pier, a joint state and federal project to provide a structure to support the pipe carrying wastewater from the old treatment plant out well beyond the surf line and to offer recreational ocean fishing, was completed in 1973. On July 25, 1978, it was renamed the Reverend Herschel Harkins Memorial Pier in honor of the long-time Presbyterian pastor of the Little Brown Church. The pier is no longer used for wastewater purposes, but it continues to bring fishermen from miles around.

During World War II, this first post office in Pacifica stood on the northwest corner of the intersection of San Jose and Palmetto Avenues, a site now vacant that serves as the annual Fog Fest sand sculpture contest venue. Later post offices existed at Pacific Manor, on the corner of Francisco Boulevard and Santa Maria Avenue, in Rockaway Beach, in Pedro Valley, and on Pedro Point before being consolidated into the main office on Manor Drive and the branch at Roberts Road.

Ocean Shore Railroad attorney Henry McCloskey built this castle in 1908 as an ultra-sturdy reassurance for his wife Emily after the shock of the 1906 earthquake. It was designed to resemble her childhood home in Scotland. One of Henry's sons, former congressman Pete McCloskey's father, occupied one of the turrets in his high school years. The castle passed through a number of hands after Henry's death in 1914. The final owner, theater painter Sam Mazza, willed the property and the extensive inventory of artifacts he had collected to the Sam Mazza Foundation for use by nonprofit organizations.

Joseph Comerford, son of immigrant British agricultural expert Michael Comerford, built this three-story mansion on the bluff near Milagra Creek surrounded by trees as windbreaks to protect the gardens. The third-floor ballroom saw memorable social events. Joseph's daughter Lydia married one of the Fahey farming family, who unfortunately died young. Lydia lived on in the mansion, gaining notoriety in 1905 by holding off Ocean Shore Railroad surveyors with a shotgun until they got proper permission to proceed. The mansion was demolished to make way for Pacific Skies Estates.

In the 1950s, the Mori Point shoreline was substantially westward of where it is now. The sandy projection on the left sheltered a small tidal estuary. Especially lively during Prohibition years, the Mori's Point Inn suffered fines and whiskey confiscation when raided. In 1953, Doug Hart took over the operation from the Moris, and he continued until 1965, when county health officials had him jailed for chronic failure to respond to sanitation citations. The inn burned down in June 1966, despite frantic efforts to bring water from nearby Fairway Park to douse the flames.

Stefano Mori and his wife, Marie, arrived from Italy about 1880 and bought a 19-acre parcel nestled beneath Mori Point. They raised crops such as artichokes and brussels sprouts and grazed goats, cattle, and a few horses. As they prospered, they enlarged their farmhouse to accommodate the farmhands and then converted the lower floor into a popular restaurant offering such specialties as homemade cheeses, sausages, and artichoke fritters. The Moris introduced the style of cheese making that became known as Jack cheese.

Dick and Victoria Plate bought land on the corner of Paloma Avenue and Old County Road in 1931. The parcel included a building believed to have been constructed by Henry McCloskey in 1909. The Plates turned it into a general grocery store called County Road Market. Descendants continued to operate it as a general store until they sold it to the current owners, who operate an antique store there. The separate wing next door has been Dick's Café, Al's Café (leased by Al Sohl and Otto Herling), a liquor store, a surf shop, and now an art gallery.

Salada Avenue in the 1920s still had only a few buildings: the Little Brown Church, two cottages owned by Downey Harvey, the Salada Hotel, and two or three houses toward the beach. The expected boom had not materialized, and growth remained slow in Salada Beach for most of the next 25 years. Post–World War II growth consisted of many young families attracted by affordable homes close to larger population centers.

This vista point along Sharp Park Road was built in May 1971 and named in honor of Grace McCarthy, longtime Girl Scout leader, Pacifica councilwoman, three-time mayor, and member of the original California Coastal Commission. It is a popular spot for watching sunsets.

VALLEMAR AND
ROCKAWAY BEACH

VALLEMAR MANOR
MRS. J. C. B. HEBBARD, Host

George Rich Sr. envisioned Vallemar as vacation homes in a park-like setting. He planted trees from many parts of the world, creating a virtual arboretum. Vallemar Manor, on the corner of Bonita and Reina Del Mar Avenues, was a hotel during the Ocean Shore Railroad days before becoming the Rich family home. It was demolished in 1960.

Glum citizens inspect some of the debris thrown up by the ocean onto Rockaway Beach Boulevard in 1958. Long experience with occasional devastating waves taught the value of sturdy barriers to owners of homes and businesses along the waterfront. In addition to the strengthened seawall, the front of Nick's Restaurant is now protected by a row of posts along the width of the building.

The Vallemar Volunteer Fire Department operated out of this station. Along with other units in Edgemar, Sharp Park, Rockaway Beach, Pedro Valley, and Pedro Point, volunteers provided fire protection until conversion to full-time status began in 1953. They were supported by assessment fees and by fund-raisers such as barbecues and whist parties. The former Vallemar firehouse is now a residence on Reina Del Mar Avenue.

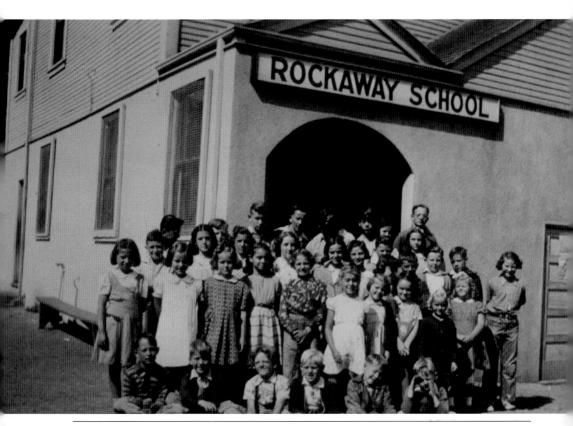

Rockaway School was built in 1914 as part of the Tobin School District. This district covered the area from Vallemar south to Devil's Slide and was named after the San Francisco banking family that had holdings in San Pedro Valley and the railroad. The two-story building had two classrooms and two teachers. The building still stands as a private residence.

In this 1958 photograph of the Rockaway Beach intersection, the railroad station is gone. Louise's Store was demolished in 1969, but the Shell station and the building that was variously the Rockaway Beach Volunteer Fire Department, the Rockaway Progressive Club, an insurance office, and now a nail-care salon remain. During commute hours, this intersection is one of the busiest in town, as many drivers choose to come down Fassler Avenue from the eastern sections of Linda Mar.

The Rockaway Station was on the east side of the Ocean Shore Railroad tracks near the present intersection of Fassler Avenue and Highway 1. It may have been torn down when the tracks were taken up and sold after 1920. Louise's Store was demolished when Fassler Avenue was widened and the lower section shifted to come into the Highway 1 intersection along with Rockaway Beach Boulevard. The Rockaway Progressive Club is behind the Shell Station.

The water tower for refilling tanks of steam locomotives was on the siding near Rockaway Station just north of Rockaway Beach Boulevard. This section of the old right-of-way is now part of Highway 1 parallel to the frontage road Harvey Way, named for H. Downey Harvey, president of the Ocean Shore Railroad when it ceased operations in 1920.

The Rockaway Progressive Club (RPC) was a political action group consisting of Nick Gust, Florence Graziani, and other concerned citizens who met in the old Rockaway Beach Volunteer Firehouse, which they owned. They opposed the incorporation of Pacifica, believing that the change would bring higher expenses without a significant improvement in governance. When they disbanded, the RPC donated the building to the new city for municipal use; they were sorely disappointed when the city later sold it.

Last productive in 1986 after its limestone was extracted to make concrete for Highway 380 (the Quentin Kopp Freeway), the Rockaway quarry has several times been the proposed site for projects such as a casino or a hotel and conference center with residential and commercial elements. Those proposals were all denied by voters, and once again the property is up for sale.

A notable eatery on the Rockaway Beach waterfront was the Breakers. Often inconvenienced by rogue waves before the seawall was built up, the Breakers was severely damaged during storms in 1958, and its owners gave up and sold the business. The attractive, if risky, site became home to the Lighthouse Hotel and Moonraker Restaurant. The hotel is now part of the Best Western hotel chain, and the restaurant is now Ristorante Portofino.

Motorcycle clubs used to be quite active in Pacifica, holding hill-climbing events on the Sharp Park and Vallemar sides of Mori Point and on Pedro Mountain south of Pedro Point. Most of the larger pine and cypress trees now growing on Mori Point between Highway 1 and the west end of the Fairway Park neighborhood were planted by the motorcyclists to screen the noise of their activities.

This vintage photograph of Mori Ridge from the south side shows the Ocean Shore Railroad right-of-way coming through Schoolhouse Cut and the farming section from Reichling Avenue to the highway where flowers and vegetables grew. Today the foreground is occupied by a new tertiary wastewater treatment plant powered by the banks of solar cells on the roof and the restored banks of Calera Creek.

The vicissitudes of Vallemar Station have been many over the years—a sometime residence, site of several restaurants, and victim of neglect, fire damage, and bankruptcy. But for some years now, it has been a successful restaurant and sports bar whose operators, Hal and Barbara Ash, have filled the interior with a fine collection of historical railroad photographs and artifacts.

One of the few unchanged features of Rockaway Beach is the desolation of the quarry. The rest of west Rockaway Beach has fared better, with modern lodgings, stores, and business offices constructed with the tax advantage of being designated a redevelopment district. Early plat maps showed an additional street to the west of the current seawall, and in 1972, a marina was proposed for the area below the quarry.

This lovely touring car parked in Nick's parking lot in Rockaway is symbolic of changes that were occurring rapidly in American life. In the background is the railroad cut where the defunct Ocean Shore Railroad used to bring holiday seekers to the coast. The age of the automobile had arrived, and life would never be the same.

The Rockaway seawall has had to be strengthened more than once since this 1968 photograph. The most recent improvement followed an incident one Sunday morning on February 22, 1998, when a tremendous wave swept ashore with such force that it smashed in the front of Nick's Restaurant. The intrepid Gust family and staff mopped up and were able to serve brunch on the dance floor, the carpets still being brine-soaked.

4

LINDA MAR AND PEDRO POINT

Until the early 1970s, the California Department of Transportation's master plan included extending the freeway section of Highway 1 through Pacifica and down the coast. This is an architect's rendering of how the highway might have looked as it swept through the south end of town. Advent of the California Coastal Commission and actions of numerous environmental advocates significantly curtailed expansion of the highway.

Artichokes flourished in San Pedro Valley almost down to the beach. The shallow marsh called Lake Mathilde had been partially filled to make agriculture possible in this area. This farm is now the Linda Mar Shopping Center. Until flood control on San Pedro Creek, this area flooded every 10 years or so. In stormy 1962, surfboards, rowboats, and a war surplus amphibious truck were used to rescue inundated residents.

The view from Alma Heights was mainly of artichoke fields in the early 1950s. Soon Andy Oddstad would purchase seven farms in one weekend as a major step toward his plans to build Linda Mar. Now the view consists of some of the buildings and playing fields of Alma Heights Christian Academy. Beyond them is the Rosita Road neighborhood.

At one time, sheep safely grazed on ranch land in the back of Pedro Valley, sometimes called "Sun Valley." However, a growing population needed room to expand, and the ranches were doomed. In 1961, Terra Nova became Pacifica's first high school. Designed by Falk and Booth, it had a modern look, and it has produced many fine scholars and athletes. It is currently being renovated and retrofitted. Additions to the campus will include a new stadium and a state-of-the-art theater.

San Pedro Valley lacked schoolhouses when the coastal elementary student population surged toward 10,000 as many young couples moved into their Linda Mar "ranchers." Seeing the need for a stopgap solution, developer Andy Oddstad removed some of the interior walls from a row of new houses and connected them with breezeways to form the first Oddstad School. They were replaced by a regular school structure for a time, but when student population later declined, the school was replaced by these new modern homes.

Tucked back in San Pedro Valley Park are remains of John Gay's trout farm. Visible in the south picnic area are the top of the walls of two tanks where fingerling trout grew large enough to be placed in the main pond along the south fork of San Pedro Creek. A local attraction for many years, the facility was so badly damaged by flooding in October 1962 that Gay closed the business. San Mateo County later acquired the property from the North Coast County Water District for use as a park.

Pacifica Community Television, now known as Channel 26, traces its roots back to the early 1960s, giving it the distinction of being the oldest continually running public access station in the United States. The crew in 1992 was filming the installation of the all-female Pacifica government—another Pacifica milestone. Today volunteer crews from Channel 26 still actively broadcast the city council meetings as well as the planning commission and school board while maintaining a full schedule of award-winning arts, entertainment, and public service programming.

The local Ocean Shore Railroad station went by various names: San Pedro Terrace by the Sea, Pedro Valley, and finally, Tobin. As the vintage image shows, it was initially a stone structure with open sides and a distinctive curved roof. While named the Pedro Valley Railroad Station, walls were added. In 1982, the exotic roof blew off, and to save money, a more conventional roof was added. It is currently a private residence.

Shelter Cove is an isolated 17-acre beachfront community started in the early 1900s as a recreation destination for San Franciscans, many who arrived on the Ocean Shore Railroad. It was a haven for bootleggers during Prohibition. It was a privately owned enclave, sometimes featuring a restaurant and cabins, and until 1975, always open to the public. Today the homes are private rentals and the public is not invited. The road around the point washed out in 1983 and is now only accessible via boat or a steep climb.

Pacifica State Beach, originally called San Pedro Beach, attracts people from all over the San Francisco Bay area. The original public showers and change rooms were dedicated in the 1950s. They were replaced by a new Spanish-style facility in 2006 as part of a project that included enlarging the parking lots and extending the handicapped-accessible Coastal Trail from Sharp Park Beach south to Linda Mar Boulevard.

LINDA MAR AND PEDRO POINT

Harry Danmann's Cliff House was built in 1908 to serve as a hotel and bar for the Ocean Shore Railroad passengers. Pictured on his front porch, Danmann was an important resident of Pedro Valley and served 50 years on the school board. After he died in 1954, the bar became Danmann's Hayloft, and it remained not just a bar but also an institution. It burned down in 1970. Today the site is a private residence with a wonderful view.

The Vagabond was a popular eatery of the 1960s and 1970s renowned for its beef dinners. The building itself started as a rendering plant on the beach. In the 1920s, it was moved to Pedro Avenue and turned into a restaurant. During Prohibition, its location close to the beach made it perfect as a place to store and serve liquor. After much renovation and change of ownership, it is again a popular eatery, Barolo's Italian Cuisine.

The Wander Inn's popular slogan was "wander in, stagger out." Located on the ocean at the end of Crespi Drive, it was a popular watering hole with spectacular ocean views from its barroom stools. It burned down in 1970. Its prime location made it a target for development, but that all came to an end when it became part of the Linda Mar State Beach. In the modern photograph, a parade of surfers is seen marching past the old stone entrance to the parking lot.

Construction began on the Sanchez Adobe in 1842, during the Mexican Rancho era. During the next 100 years, the adobe was used as a hotel, a bordello, a hunting lodge, an artichoke packing shed, and farm laborers' quarters. Ray Mori operated a speakeasy in the adobe during Prohibition. In 1953, restoration was begun by San Mateo County, and today the restored Sanchez Adobe is a popular tourist attraction.

As the post–World War II baby boomers grew up, the population of school-age children declined, and the Laguna Salada School District was faced with surplus schools. When Sanchez School was offered to public agencies for 24 percent of its assessed value per California law, the City of Pacifica bought it. A grassroots effort eventually turned the formerly run-down campus into the Pacifica Center for the Arts, home to Mildred Owen Concert Hall, the Sanchez Art Center, sports fields, a fine art photography studio, and a credit union.

The vantage point of the vintage photograph is overlooking San Pedro Beach in the 1950s. Toward the far end of the beach, Crespi Drive and Wander Inn are visible. In the foreground is Danmann Avenue with the water tower, old railroad station, old Pedro Point Post Office, and Danmann's Hayloft. Today the view is partially blocked by trees. The firehouse is still there, as well as some new private homes and live-work spaces. Linda Mar Beach has lost a few homes, and the distant Pacifica Beach Hotel is a handsome addition.

The Long Table Restaurant opened in 1964 in what was then called the Sea Village Shopping Center on the west side of Highway 1. This smorgasbord-style restaurant could seat 400 people and was open from 11:00 a.m. to 11:00 p.m. daily. Lunches cost $1 and dinners $1.50. The restaurant was adjacent to a Safeway that had opened in 1963. Today three popular restaurants fill this spot in Pedro Point: the Wave Café, La Playa, and Nonas's Kitchen.

Pedro Point's isolation attracted many unique individuals and other footloose and beachcomber types, water lovers, boaters, artists, and surfers. After World War II, when the water supply was assured, the area also attracted home buyers who admired the sweeping views northward along the coast to San Francisco and beyond to Point Reyes. Today some small charming old cottages still exist, but the new homes being built are very grand and take advantage of the spectacular views.

The first St. Peter's Catholic Church in Pacifica was in this modified garage on the corner of Adobe and Rosita Drives. The accompanying house served as the rectory. Previously, the local congregation met in the Rockaway Mission Church, an extension of Holy Angels Church in Colma, on Rockaway Beach Boulevard. Now minus the small steeple, the building serves as a day care center.

This is one of the earliest views ever published of Pedro Point, although the feature often appeared on early nautical charts. This wood engraving appeared in an illustrated book called *Picturesque America* published by William Cullen Bryant in 1872. The two-volume book was considered a masterpiece and helped to raise awareness of the hidden beauty in America. Although more than 100 years have passed, the view has not changed significantly.

Imagine a drive-up beach party on a hot day at San Pedro Beach in the 1950s. The rough-paved area in the center of the old photograph may have been part of the Ocean Shore Railroad's Fleming Station shown on early maps. The slabs in the lower part of the photograph were part of the Wander Inn property. Little evidence remains of the old structures now.

Discover Thousands of Local History Books
Featuring Millions of Vintage Images

Arcadia Publishing, the leading local history publisher in the United States, is committed to making history accessible and meaningful through publishing books that celebrate and preserve the heritage of America's people and places.

Find more books like this at
www.arcadiapublishing.com

Search for your hometown history, your old stomping grounds, and even your favorite sports team.

Consistent with our mission to preserve history on a local level, this book was printed in South Carolina on American-made paper and manufactured entirely in the United States. Products carrying the accredited Forest Stewardship Council (FSC) label are printed on 100 percent FSC-certified paper.

MADE IN THE USA